SILENT
VOICES

AN ANTHOLOGY
OF
ROMANIAN
WOMEN POETS

translated
by
ANDREA DELETANT
and
BRENDA WALKER

with an introduction
by
FLEUR ADCOCK

FOREST BOOKS
LONDON   1986   BOSTON

PUBLISHED BY FOREST BOOKS
20 Forest View, Chingford, London E4 7AY, U.K.
61 Lincoln Road, Wayland, M.A. 01788, U.S.A.

First published 1986

Typeset in Great Britain by Cover to Cover, Cambridge
Printed in Great Britain by A. Wheaton & Co Ltd, Exeter

Translations © Andrea Deletant, Brenda Walker

British Library Cataloguing in Publication Data
Silent voices: an anthology of contemporary
Romanian women poets.
1. Romanian poetry—Translations into English
2. English poetry—Translations from Romanian
3. Romanian poetry—Women authors.
I. Deletant, Andrea   II. Walker, Brenda
859". 134"0809287   PC871.E3
ISBN 0 948259 03 5

Library of Congress Catalog Card Number
85–080386

Acknowledgements

Poems in this anthology have been taken from the following volumes:

FLORENTA ALBU
EPITAF (1983) *Cartea Românească, Bucureşti*
TERASE (1983) *Cartea Românească, Bucureşti*

MARIA BANUS
OROLOGIU CU FIGURI (1984) *Editura Eminescu, Bucureşti*
TOCMAI IESEAM DIN ARENA (1967)

ANA BLANDIANA
ORA DE NISIP (1983) *Editura Eminescu, Bucureşti*
OCTOMBRIE, NOIEMBRIE, DECEMBRIE (1972)
Cartea Românească, Bucureşti
SOMNUL DIN SOMN (1977) *Cartea Românească, Bucureşti*

CONSTANTA BUZEA
POEME (1977) *Editura Albatros, Bucureşti*
PLOI DE PIATRA (1979) *Editura Albatros, Bucureşti*
UMBRA PENTRU CER (1981) *Editura Albatros, Bucureşti*
PLANTA MEMORIEI (1985) *Cartea Românească, Bucureşti*

NINA CASSIAN
DE INDURARE (1893) *Editura Eminescu, Bucureşti*
NUMARATOAREA INVERSA (1983) *Editura Eminescu, Bucureşti*

DENISA COMANESCU
IZGONIREA DIN PARADIS (1979) *Editura Cartea Românească, Bucureşti*
CUTITUL DE ARGINT (1983) *Editura Eminescu, Bucureşti*
URMA FOCULUI (1986) *Editura Eminescu, Bucureşti*

IOANA CRACIUNESCU
IARNA CLINICA (1983) *Editura Cartea Românească, Bucureşti*
MASINARIA CU ABURI (1984) *Editura Eminescu, Bucureşti*

DANIELA CRASNARU
CRINGUL HIPNOTIC (1979) *Editura Eminescu, Bucureşti*
NIAGARA DE PLUMB (1984) *Editura Eminescu, Bucureşti*

CAROLINA ILICA
TIRANIA VISULUI (1982) *Editura Cartea Românească, Bucureşti*
TIRANIA VISULUI (1985) *Editura Eminescu, Bucureşti*

ILEANA MALANCIOIU
LINIA VIETTI (1982) *Editura Cartea Românească, Bucureşti*
URCAREA MUNTELIU (1985) *Editura Albatros, Bucureşti*

ANGELA MARINESCU
BLINDAJUL FINAL (1981) *Editura Cartea Românească, Bucureşti*

GRETE TARTLER
SCRISORI DE ACREDITARE (1982) *Editura Eminescu, Bucureşti*
SUBSTITUIRI (1983) *Editura Cartea Românească, Bucureşti*

DOINA URICARIU
NATURA MOARTA CU SUFLET (1982) *Editura Eminescu, Bucureşti*
MINA PE FATA (1984) *Editura Cartea Românească, Bucureşti*

LILIANA URSU
VIATA DEASUPRA ORASULUI (1977) *Editura Cartea Românească, Bucureşti*
PIATA AURARILOR (1980) *Editura Cartea Românească, Bucureşti*
ZONA DE PROTECTIE (1983)*Editura Eminescu, Bucureşti*

Contents

Introduction

Romanian poetry has a flavour of its own which can be experienced even in translation. It shares certain qualities (notably an inclination towards fable, allegory and extended metaphor) with the poetry of its East European neighbours, but it also has its own clear individuality. This has in part grown out of the language itself, a Romance language derived from Latin and kept alive, in spite of the powerful forces which threatened it, for two thousand years. The other Romance languages (French, Italian, Spanish) had a relatively easy passage through the centuries, since their countries bordered upon each other and mutual understanding was not impossible, but the Romanian people were linguistically isolated and subject to constant pressures from outside. Although their language now contains Slavonic, Turkish and other elements which bear witness to its history, its basic fabric has not been eroded. The survival of the language confirms and symbolizes the survival of the nation itself, and the strong identity of the Romanian people has much to do with this continued refusal to surrender to any linguistic takeover.

In the twentieth century Romanian literature has, of course, been influenced by the currents of international literary fashion, but this has been part of a process of give and take, with Romanian writers contributing their own particular ideas and enthusiasms to European culture. Tristan Tzara, the inventor of Dadaism, was Romanian, as were some of the early Surrealists and the playwright Eugene Ionescu, a pioneer of the 'Theatre of the Absurd'. These movements have had their day, but they have left traces on the work of succeeding writers; Romanian poetry is still given to fantasy, irony, and bursts of startling inventiveness.

The poetry in this book is recent, and reflects the relaxation in Romanian cultural attitudes which occurred in the 1960s. It can never be entirely easy for poets to write in a society where publishing is subject to state control, but poetry is enormously popular in Romania, and its practitioners are welcomed and respected. The variety of styles and techniques to be found in present-day Romanian poetry shows the continuing vigour of the art. There is a new generation of postwar poets (most of those included in this collection were born in the 1940s or 1950s) who have managed to express themselves with passion and grace no matter what constraints they may operate under. It is particularly encouraging that so many of the younger poets are women. The extent to which women's poetry differs stylistically from that written by men—if indeed it differs at all—is a matter of controversy; but what is interesting (and perhaps even more important when the poems are to be read in translation) is the range of themes covered by women poets. It is not surprising that a woman should write well about mother-hood (I am thinking, for example, of Doina Uricariu's savagely tender poetry about breast-feeding her baby, and Ana Blandiana's moving and extraordinary poem *Pietá*, which indirectly presents the Virgin Mary as an archetype of the mother who never ceases to be maternal even when her child is grown up); but I was also impressed by the tenderness and power with which some of these poets write about childhood and old age. Maria Banus combines both themes in *Amazing*, where she describes the naked, unprotected feeling that results from losing one's own parents, ramparts against the world's dangers, and becoming the protector oneself:

> *Now I'm the rampart*
> *nothing protects me*
> *from the cold which keeps rising*
> *I'll stay here for a while*
> *to cover the emptiness lying ahead of the children.*

Banuş is the oldest poet included here, and is able to write about old age not only from observation (as do Florenţa Albu, Liliana Ursu and others) but from the inside, as it were. Her stark, honest descriptions of what it means to be growing weaker and more helpless have little cheer in them, but there is a singing moment in *The Lost Child* where she wakes from a frightening dream of being young again and rejoices at being simply alive:

> *It's morning. I'm seventy.*
> *Humble ecstasy of being.*

Next in seniority to Banuş is Nina Cassian, a prolific and justly admired poet with a body of mature work to choose from. Her uncompromising poems about the loss of love refuse to countenance any spirit of resignation but tingle with unsubdued passion and rage: see, for example, her brilliantly grisly *Donna Miraculata*, where the deserted woman sees herself as 'a corpse lighting up the darkness', with hands like rags and a 'halo of decay' shining on her temples. But she has also written vividly about her childhood, as in *Part of a Bird*, a wonderfully sensuous evocation of a summer by the sea, with its joyful picture of the physical lightness and apparent invulnerability of a healthy child:

> *. . . and if I wasn't flying*
> *it was only because I preferred to run on earth*
> *and not for any other reason.*

Family life also finds its way into some of these poems; Denisa Comănescu, in *Family Portrait*, sees the humour of it (although the mood of this poem takes a sharp turn towards tragedy at the end). Ileana Mălăncioiu, in *Love Story*, wittily introduces death as a metaphor for the decay of a relationship, perhaps a marriage:

> *Everything began with great enthusiasm*
> *I would have died without you, you without me*
> *When suddenly we both died I don't know how*
> *And on a day so frantically busy.*

Liliana Ursu also seems to be writing of marriage in several of her hauntingly frozen, locked-in poems, with their sense of suspended animation and a paralysed inability to act. Aspects of love recur throughout the book, treated in a variety of modes of which I shall mention here only the curious, obscurely erotic poems of Ioana Crăciunescu, with their unexpected images and gritty vigour of language (*With Blouse Undone*, which *may* be about polishing furniture, strikes me as a miniature gem of ambiguity).

Personal concerns may predominate in this selection, but these poets are women with careers and wide interests, and they also address social, moral and philosophical questions. Several of them (Banuş, Mălăncioiu, Ursu) use the image of a theatrical performance as a metaphor for public life or human existence in general. This idea is most thoroughly exploited by Daniela Crăsnaru, in her clever satires *The Stage Dressing Room* and *The Rehearsal Studio*, whose lively, colloquial surface effects and witty asides do not conceal the undercurrent of despair which flows beneath them. Another of her poems, *Everything is for Our Own Good*, gives a rather more sombre picture of the desperation felt by an individual living in the crowded, insecure, technologically threatening world of the late twentieth century.

Other poets who confront such issues are Liliana Ursu, with her bleak vignette of an eternally repeated bureaucratic existence in *Circuit*, and Grete Tartler, whose chilling little fable *Didactica Nova*, about a child who does not conform to the expectations of an unimaginative and heartless teacher, is a powerful parable of the individual unjustly treated by authority:

> . . . *How many fingers have you got on one hand?*
> *Five, replied the child.*
> *Well, how many on two hands?*
> *Eleven, comes the answer.*
> *The blows fall. On the hand with five fingers.*
> *On the hand*
> *with six.*

The fourteen poets included here are very different in their styles and approaches, but there are enough threads of similarity to reveal their common background and their links with one another. Visual details here and there (the factually convincing glimpses of urban life, the occasional folk-art quality of some of the rural settings, the snowy landscapes—Romanian has at least two quite separate words for different states of snow) remind us that these poems were written in Romanian; while the more intimate and inwardly-focussed areas of the poetry make it clear that these women have insights and experiences to share with women everywhere.

Fleur Adcock

FLORENTA ALBU was born in December 1934 in the county of Ialomița. She graduated from the Faculty of Philology at Bucharest University and her first volume of poems appeared in 1961. Her eleventh and most recent collection was published in 1985. She now works as editor of the poetry section on the literary review *Viața Românească*.

GOLDEN WEDDING

They, bridal pair of winter,
we, snowed in
at the wedding of parents,
we so very old
giving testimony
at the wedding of our parents.

The earth soothed under footsteps
with a cry, with a fading out.

They pass under the horizon
together, hand in hand,
golden bridal pair,
with a stoop of gold,
with faces of gold,
wheat crowns of gold
special clothes chosen,
wedded in heaven,
the only ones to plight their troth
on the field of ice,
John and Mary, servants of earth
on the field of ice.

Florenţa Albu

FACES

The wind beats old faces, behind the windows.
Where are you from, sad ones, single ones?
What are you saying, in the wind,
what are you laughing at with toothless mouths?

Rope-coloured hair, thin and blown by the wind,
old hair, old grey,
—what alive tiredness
from long ago, from the villages.

People came just the same on the roads.
A sunset. And tiredness drained away
with the sun, in clumps.
Yellow corn. And peasant shoes. Backpacks.
The colour of disease. Colour of living ghosts
pacing the middle of a field.
—Where are you coming from, Fear?
A yellow face. The last in the window.
Yet insisting. Still insisting.

I'm going back. There in memory.
On the tracks of memory.
Near the mulberry trees and hostility.
—What are your names? I ask children at the crossroads.
They scatter, with small unfriendly
faces,—hostile faces—
My own face—a child's, unfriendly
and hostile.

OLD PRAYER

Bells, wind, bells
Spring, death, resurrection—
God give us rain—
God give us sun—

the rotation of the earth in a seed—

God give us rain
God give us sun
and rain in time
and time in time;

patience to start again from the beginning—
to sow,
to let yourself be crucified,
buried, resurrected—

God give us rain,
God give us sun,
God give us rain in time
and time in time.

OLD CHILDREN

The children are almost old, almost
tired. They come to the village,
stay near the porch.
Dusk sets in.
They wait.
Night falls.
They wait.

Sometimes it seems that children from long ago
pass through the fields.
Lights from pumpkins
poke tongues at the stars:
chasing each other
on the narrow way.
Aping each other
aping us,
not wanting to come home.
Mother no longer sees them.
Father no longer hears them.
They no longer answer to our names.

SUMMER

Especially this summer
burned without glory
without memories
an old mirage
crossing its arms
on the foundation of air . . .

Torrid days.
Time tramps
with boots of the reformed
through the gardens of our love.

The Daily—if only I could detach myself
finally
from it—that precise hungry
Daily!

The garden of our loves . . .
The light heart of the falling fruit . . .
That precise hungry Daily . . .

THE AGONY

Listen to
the town in the evenings
the life/voices
the swishing of cars on a wet surface
the calling of magpies from somewhere or other—
the agony!
To listen to your agony
here and now: that agony—

the feeling of a sonorous incision
the curious amazed
intrusion
illumination with darkness

and even your blood—you know
doesn't belong to you
it comes from far away to you
bequeathed to you
with this agony—

Your aims's to perfect it
to hand it on
the complete code/the essence.

THE SCARECROW

A long night in heaven and on earth—
I lose myself in heaven and on earth.

A new year in the old nut tree
the scarecrow dressed up for New Year
in my ball gown
(I never had one but dreamed of it
at eighteen . . .)
and the veil in the wind
and an egret's feather
and a glove thrown down in the wind.

The scarecrow in the walnut tree
let's imagine it once again
and in the place reserved for scarecrows
let's raise this one
Self in the sky
even in the rotating drunken zodiac

—let's wave to it
foretell its fate
scarecrow of the new year—

there in the north wind
Miss Me
provokes the emptiness with the left
glove.

MARIA BANUS made her debut at the age of 14 in 1928 when Tudor Arghezi published her first poem in his satirical journal *'Bilete de papagal'*. A graduate in Philology and Law, her first collection appeared in 1937 and she has been published regularly since then. Her verse of the fifties reflected the cultural dictates of the period, but her later work (published in many volumes of poetry over the years) is distinguished by its variety. In addition to several volumes of essays she has translated from the work of Goethe, Rilke, Browning and Pushkin.

Maria Banuş

SEPARATION

My name has torn away from me,
crossed the ford, is on the other side,
through autumn wind
through rivers of leaves
we're only just in earshot

fleetingly I see it
sizing me up
from the other shore
with its guilty and ironic smile

while I grow smaller and smaller
crouched knees to the forehead
in Autumn's womb

NATURAL

You pull this way, I pull that
you're all flood and frenzy
I—all logic and melancholy

what a couple we make—oh God
what unnatural obscene coupling
a painting of laughter and dread

yet how splendidly
and with what demented art
are the details refined

US, YORICK

Without complexes let's embark
on that used metaphor
a ship the shape of a skull
to navigate on luminous waves
of the brain
us, Yorick
the good jester
us who bombard
the court of Elsinore
with words to puzzle over
people fidgeting and laughing
Claudius plunged into action
giving us a kick
to jolt us a bit
so as not to upset
his ingenious plans with light-hearted words
not to halt his tragi-comedy in its path

it moves on ahead
but we don't give up
uttering fearful words
forecasts hiding nothing
and hiding where Polonius dies—
while the garland of flowers
while the swords
while the goblets of poison . . .

AMAZING

Amazing
so small and weak
and yet a rampart
no one could get past you
nor could we see clearly
what was hidden behind you
there where it all fell
walking sticks and hats
sewing machines and embroidered bedspreads.

Now I'm the rampart
nothing protects me
from the cold which keeps rising
I'll stay here for a while
to cover the emptiness lying ahead of the children

THE LOST CHILD

Panic in my dream:
God, I can't be forty,
I'm still a child.
How have I failed you?

I wake up.
Light filters through the blinds.
It's morning. I'm seventy.
Humble ecstasy of being.

Maria Banuş

MIGRATION

A hand comes with the spoon
to please our tongues
a hand comes with the pliers
to pull out our tongues
a hand comes close
another vanishes

the sky—full of rustling hands
of birds coming and going
following laced leaping laws

THE TREE

The hands couldn't hold anything anymore
the glass falling—breaking
then you'd sewn so many pockets
on your house-coat
putting:
keys in one
a glass in another
a spoon in another
one hand on the walking stick
the other leaning on the furniture
staying like that
a century
between one step and another
a dried up tree
full of empty, black walnuts,
of sleigh bells faintly tinkling

TIME

Clench your fists woman
I can't
there's nothing you can do
time
advances slowly
I move forwards
under the sumptuous angle
of the storks
in the October velvet
I lean gently
with stiff fingers
on the shoulder
of my seductive killer

THE WEDDING

In the bridal suite there was a black, cosmic cold.

Get undressed, I told him—to warm me.

First he unscrewed his head,
with the grinding of Saturn,
when it wants to escape the grip of the ring
or like a glass stopper,
which grates against the neck of a bottle.
He unscrewed his right arm,
like a pin from a grenade.
He unscrewed his left arm
like a slender metallic rocket.
He unscrewed his artificial limb from his right leg,
swearing like a mechanic at a broken-down engine,
he unscrewed his artificial limb from his left leg,
and iron groaned upon iron,
as it does in a boiler room.

I crawled near his heart,
put my head on his chest,
listened to his heart-beat.

It wasn't grinding, or clanging, or exploding,
it was throbbing—

Blades of grass grew, unexpectedly,
the face of a hare appeared from hazel branches,
a milky strip of cloud—and a sky.
Then, finally, we cried.

EIGHTEEN

The streets are wet. Large drops have rained like money,
silver, or gold coins by the handful.
My mind charges at the world like a bull.
Today's my eighteenth birthday.

With mad thoughts soft rain beats against me.
Look, how its beads run slowly, warmly,
like wet nappies clinging tightly,
when left for an hour unchanged.

Yes, it's rained like tomorrow, like yesterday, or forever,
the heart is one, the heart forages ever further.
Like temples of time, my temple throbs loudly.

I'm thinking of drinking life like so many do,
but even the strong vapour of the sap—burns me.
You see today's my eighteen birthday.

ANA BLANDIANA was born in 1942 in Timişoara. She attended secondary school in Oradea and in 1967 graduated from Cluj University in Philology. After serving as an editor on the literary journals *Viaţa Românească* and *Amfiteatru* she worked as a librarian at the Institute of Fine Arts in Bucharest. She is now a freelance writer. Her first volume of verse appeared in 1964. She has a regular column in the Union of Writers weekly *România Literară* and is also the author of several children's books.

THE COUPLE

Some see only you,
Others see only me,
We superimpose so perfectly
That no-one can spot us at the same time
And no-one dares to live on the edge
From where we can both be seen.
You see only the moon,
I see only the sun,
You yearn for the sun,
I yearn for the moon,
But we stay back to back,
Bones united long ago,
Our blood carries rumours
From one heart to the other.
What are you like?
I lift my arm
And stretch backwards
I discover your sweet shoulder-blade
And, going upwards, the fingers touch
Your divine lips,
Then suddenly return
To crush my mouth, bleeding.
What are we like?
We have four arms for defence
But only I can hit the enemy here
And only you the enemy there,
We have four legs to run,
But you can only run on your side
And I on mine.
Every step's a life and death struggle.
How equal are we?
Are we to die together or will one of us carry,
For a time
The corpse of the other stuck to our side

Infecting with death, slowly, too slowly,
Or perhaps never to die completely
But carry for an eternity
The sweet burden of the other,
Atrophied forever,
The size of a hunch,
The size of a wart . . .
Oh, only we know the longing
To look into each other's eyes
And so at last understand,
But we stay back to back,
Grown like two branches
And if one should tear away,
Sacrificing all for a single look,
You would only see of the other
The back from which you came
Bleeding, shivering,
Tearing.

DO YOU REMEMBER
THE BEACH?

Do you remember the beach
Covered with painful fragments
On which
We couldn't walk barefoot,
The way
You were looking at the sea
Saying you were listening to me?
Do you remember
The frantic seagulls
Wheeling in the ringing
Of unseen church bells
Whose patron saints were fishes,
And how
You distanced yourself running
Towards the sea
Calling to me
That you needed distance
To look at me?
The falling snow
Was dying
Stirred with the birds
In the water,
With an almost happy despair
I was watching
The traces of your steps on the sea
And the sea
Was closing like an eyelid
Over the eye in which I waited.

IT'S SNOWING

It's snowing with malice,
The snow falls with hate
Above waters icy with loathing,
Above orchards blossomed by evil,
Above embittered birds who suffer,
It snows as if the aquatic dweller
Would feel this life ebbing,
It snows
With human drive,—
Venomously it's snowing.
Who then to surprise?
Only I know
That once a flurry of snow
Was love, at the beginning.—
It's so late
And hideously it's snowing,
And my mind's stopped working
So I wait
To be of use
To this wolf that's starving.

IN FALLING

First I cast
Words
One by one,
Dropped eruditely
Coupling
In falling;
Then one by one,
The years,
Distanced from each other equally,
Graded by subtle art;
Then I hurry
As in a shipwreck to cast away
All ballast,
Anything that drags me down,
Memories, wishes, passions,
Loves, and finally
When there's nothing more
To throw
Not one bit of clothing, however flimsy,
I take off my crumpled skin
And the numb flesh from the bones.
This—the great strip-tease
Which I do almost
Of my own free will.

ARMOUR

My body's
Nothing but the armour
Chosen by an archangel
For passing through this world in,
And, so disguised,
Wings packed away
Inside,
The visor of a smile
Well down over the face,
It goes to the thick of the battle,
Letting itself be hailed with filth,
Splashed with looks,
Or even caressed
On that cold breast plate of skin
Where repulsion now incubates
The exterminating angel.

CONDITIONS

I am
Like
Sand
In an hour glass
Which
Is time
Only
When
Falling.

LONELINESS

Loneliness is a town
Where everyone is dead,
Streets are clean,
Markets empty,
Everything's visible at once
Dilated in emptiness
So clearly ordained.
Loneliness is a town
Where it's snowing heavily
And not one step
Profanes the light
Laid in layers,
And only you, the wakeful eye
Open over those asleep,
See, and understand, unsatiated
With so much silence and pureness
Where none fight
Or are lied to
Where even the tear
Is too pure
To do the abandoned creature harm.
In the valley
Between suffering and death
Loneliness is a happy town.

PARENTS' LAND

My hair reached the ground
And thirty years
Seemed such a distant reward
That I never believed
I'd ever achieve it,
Full of cruelty I moved away
From Parent's land
To a world not yet invented.

It's not been invented to this day,
But now my hair's not so long,
Thirty years is just food for the way,
And I'd give it all to reach Parents' Land.

Yet Parents' Land
Is always found too late,
For everything's now desolate
And only when the moon's shining
They still meet
Under the lopped trees,
Shadows of condemned fathers
And mothers of thirty
Combing
Girls with curls
Down to the ground.

Ana Blandiana

PORTRAIT WITH CHERRIES
FOR EARRINGS

They still ripen
Near my ears
Today in pairs
Tomorrow none

Cherries so sweet
And so childlike
You're so alike
When you meet

From your shoulder
You bend easily
Counting eagerly
Leaves of clover

You still place
As in past years
Coronets of flowers
Under the quince

And under the plum
And apricot trees
With closed eyes
Still do that sum

Monday and Tuesday
Thursday with Friday
To take me away
From my heyday

And just for once
Cherries I wear
Which lie there
At my dead face

How strange the crown full
Of peonies and posies,
Pinks and roses
That rests upon my skull.

SO SIMPLE

Oh, if only I were a candle,
To waste gradually
From one end to the other,
Simply, as in sums
Of children . . .
My mind first—what happiness!—
Would disappear.
People would say
'How mindless is this girl!'
I'd remember nothing
Nor attempt to understand.
My heart would then melt
And I'd love no more,
Hate no more,
No suffering would reach me,
And people would say
'How heartless is this girl!'
And again, again
And then not one wish more
No passion,
And my blood, carrier of ships
Would scatter,
To leave only
Shrivelled knees,
Shaking with dignity or kneeling.
No one would even speak.
In the last silence,
The wax pool
Especially punished, cooled
For the horrific shadows which
Its light brought into the world.

SOMETIMES I DREAM
OF MY BODY

Sometimes I dream my body's
Caught up in wrinkled nets,
And pulled through snow
On the frozen shining shore
Of a clear sea,
I never see the fisherman
Yet I know he's your father.
I only see the net of wrinkles
And my body, a richer
Catch.
I dream wistfully of that morning of death,
A purity of peace that's strange to me
Where you no longer reach me
And I no longer call for you
And everything sleeps with open eyes
And only light in light, an echo
Will stir a fragile curse—
Untangle the nets,
To slip again
Into that pure and timeless water.

HAVE I THE RIGHT?

To reach my ancestors
Have I the right to break
The chain started from creation,
Or even long before,
From the God-amoeba,
Torn into two,
Lived in by fishes, flown by birds?
Have I the right to suddenly say
No.
To the long chain of torment
Killing me parent by parent
As far as me?

Can I return
In death amongst them
And tell them
I've left no one in my place?
Oh yes,
How else
Can I thank them
For the peace that awaits me
Other than by taking them a lasting peace
Other than by saying: It's all over,
Parents and guardians of mine,
Nothing will ever again tie you
To life now,
You're free!
And with that soft gentle touch
Children use when caressing parents,
I'd put a death-halo round their brow,
And smiling, put them with the Saints.

PIETÁ

The clear pain, the death has brought me back,
Submitted to your arms, almost a child.
You didn't know whether to be thankful
Or cry
For such happiness,
Mother.
My body, stripped of the mystery
Is yours alone.
Sweet your tears drip onto my shoulder
And gather obediently near the blade.
How good it is!
The pilgrimages and words never to be understood,
The disciples, of whom you're proud, of whom you are
                                    afraid,
The Father, the assumed, the unspoken, watching,
All is behind.
Calmed by the understood suffering
You hold me in your arms
And stealthily
You rock me, gently,
Rock me, Mama.
Three days only, I'm allowed to rest
In death and on your lap.
Then the resurrection will come
And again you are not meant to understand.
Three days only,
But until then
I feel so good
On your lap, descended from the cross,
If I wasn't afraid you'd find it terrifying,
I'd turn my mouth gently
To your breast, suckling.

CONSTANTA BUZEA was born in Bucharest in 1941. She studied Romanian at University and since 1973 she has worked as an editor for the journal *Amfiteatru*. Her first book of verse was published in 1963, since when she has written a dozen volumes. She is also the author of a number of children's books.

Constança Buzea

THERE WHERE I THINK YOU ARE

There where I think you are,
Not even trains pass,
The forests of frosty firs
Appear there like glass.

Further and further away you feel,
Always added to the rest, And still.
I cannot go forward
Unless I loose myself as well.

And all time breathes white,
Roads are white in the snow.
I wouldn't even recognise you now
Without the pair of us, without a halo.

I feel pity when remembering,
Yet can't bring myself to forget
How much illusion is in destiny,
How many mistakes can be met.

As if from under a snowed up shawl
With cold fingers I gather
Our soul, still sincere,
With its movement towards silver.

The way it snows, it may not stop,
And the firs would be encircled there,
Amongst barbarian meteorites,
There where I think you are.

Every year I wait
For the snow, so that I can see you,
See if you look, if you listen,
If you understand a little more now.

THE END OF THE WORLD

Don't let memory keep
All the words,
Our hurtful words,
Beautiful and cold.

Chosen and calmly spoken,
You hardly understand them,
Our hurtful words,
When they leave, you bury them.

There is silver and shadows of kings
At the end of the world,
Our hurtful words,
Beautiful and cold.

THE NAIVE REWARDING
OF ONE WHO LIES

The same old journeys and the same old aims,
The same old pigeons on a bowl of rice,
The naive rewarding of the one who lies.

I'm longing for rest and for Holy things,
For full and bitter tears,
For humility and for prayers
Towards the sadness of mothers' graves.

Since I'm saddled with these few words
Hanging round my neck, my mind demands
An eye for an eye, and a tooth for a tooth.

AUTOGRAPH

The author of the bill
Presents me with an autograph shadowing me
Demolishing me without so much as a word

And I could have stayed outside in the rain
Paralysed before the large windows
I could have continued to live modestly
Twiddling my fingers
In the pockets of my raincoat

Accumulating a coldness which is all mine
Would have been generous

YOU

Cloak discarded in the grass
faithfully keeping
the warmth of another body

white linen

I enter into you slowly
as to an after-death
I believe in.

MYSTERY

The wool's made me ill

I'm a weave
a thick carpet

ready to give birth
I unfold under your eyes

close them

GULF

Gentleness
with wounded angels
comes not to us
but to the invalids
we'll become

PRAYER

Come and stand by me
in the same vestments
in the same body

I won't have a moment
to watch you
or time to cry

A death-mill
crushes
and drowns me

come and stand by me
come and gratify
God

TEMPT HIM

Tempt him
Give him the taste of wild strawberries
Crush the snail in his path
Close the book
He's reading from

Tempt him
With the chirping of crickets
In the hay
Beside the birch tree place the stone
Under which we'll stay.

LONELY RIVER

I grow sombre
You're already crying

Close my eyes
Lord
Mirror of mine

Words don't assuage thirst
It stands
On the shore of the past

Lonely river
Shunned by earth

Unheard
Unmoved
Unable—
Sees mountains—
Sees you standing—
Free

NINA CASSIAN was born in 1924 in Galați. She studied drama and painting in Bucharest. One of her earliest poems was published in the Communist Party journal *România Liberă* in 1945, but her first cycle *La scara 1/1* was considered to be out of step with party ideology. Her verse of the early fifties was more in keeping with the official spirit of the time, but since the sixties she has asserted her personality in numerous outstanding collections. She is also an author of children's books and composes music. At the present time she is a visiting professor and teaches creative writing at New York University.

THAT'S ABOUT IT

More and more often,
more and more painfully,
I remember something else:
how a child once pulled faces at me,
how all the addresses where I lived
had names of plants,
the smell of my drawing book
and, after that,
the atmosphere of a kiss which embraced me,
I walked and breathed kisses to suffocation,
and, after that, sacks with the dead
which I carried on my back
and still carry
—well, yes that's it,
that's about it,
that's what you'd call my life,
the one in the skin of the sea,
in the garment of the grass,
in the curse of not speaking,
in the labour of not creating.

LIKE ANA

Once I entered with you
into a house of love
and left it fleeing
from misunderstanding,
hating the long street
and the sky without stars.
Then the first stone fell
on my heart.
Now the building's finished.
No more breathing inside.

Ana was the wife of a master builder in the Romanian legend Meşterul Manole, in which her sacrifice was required to ensure the durability of his building.

51

Nina Cassian

MORNING EXERCISES

I wake up and say: I'm through.
It's my first thought at dawn.
What a nice way to start the day
with such a murderous thought.

God, take pity on me
—is the second thought, and then
I get out of bed
and live as if
nothing had been said.

FAIRYTALE

—Why is it that the ugliest of the ugly,
the most hideous of the hideous—wants to be called
                                    Prince Charming?
—But, answered the Princess, what befits a disguise?
What if inside that scabby toad there lies bewitched
the wonderful Prince himself?
That's a risk I dare not take.

And the Princess kissed his warts
And took him to bed with her,
And the scabby toad croaked—
satisfied.

THE PROTECTOR

Again the sea without error
comes forward to meet me
the one who never deceives me
which, with its sweet armour
protects my body
from your ardour.

ACCIDENT

God protect me from those flashing knives,
Envy and malice,
Because I wake up bleeding, left huddled on tracks to die,
Just as I once found a sheep
Far more innocent than I.

WEDDING

I'm like a bride
In the house of light.

So much light
Hurts my sight.

The veil gives way
From so much light.

The ring on my finger
Breaks in the light.

And my brow's white.
A horseshoe of light

On my mouth burns—
But the thorns? The thorns?

DONNA MIRACULATA

Since you left me I seem more beautiful
Like a corpse lighting up the darkness.
My eye now more fixed and spherical
Can no longer be seen—or my carcass.

Or the rags of my hands upon objects,
or my useless walking disfigured by longing,
—Just your cruelty on my perfect temples,
Like a halo of decay that's shining.

BREAD AND WINE

We said there'd be a celebration . . .
There wasn't.
And so I dressed for no apparent
reason in the height of fashion.

I waited for you till dawn,
All night I waited.
In the carafe—stagnant wine,
on the tables—stale bread.

And when day came upon the land
—and I knew it would remain there—
I took the flowers from my hair
with a withered hand.

THE PASSION

Last night I dreamed of kissing,
Fields of ragged carnations
Sun stabbing four horizons
With its knives flashing—
From the kisses blood was dripping.

The air, warm as at a stake,
Was spreading rusty fluids;
My mouth was full of kisses,
I tried but couldn't escape—
The whole field flickered like a stake.

A forest, its green breast plate
Breathing way off, in the coolness.
Ragged carnations where my feet press
Showed me the distance I must complete
To reach that green breast plate.

And in kisses I stayed—burning.
Clouds chased by cruel sun;
I was never meant to reach them
Sheltered greens—so cooling—
I was kissing carnations—burning . . .

YOU DISTANCE YOURSELF

You distance yourself swimming, with the moon
you distance yourself, sometimes at noon,
and I'm indifferent when you're moving
a heavy arm under clouds that are weeping.

And when you rise up on the shore
And like a falling cloak your shoulders lose the sea
there's no temptation in my mind anymore
no emotion kisses me.

PART OF A BIRD

Even now my breast bone's aching
when I remember how I was running
because the smell of petunias invaded everything.
Ah, God, how warm it was around
my legs, bare, long and free
and evening fell over the sea,
over a crowd, gathered there, and over
the strange deserted pavilion
where we played and I
didn't even think about my ugly head
and other children hadn't noticed it either
because we were all running too fast instead
so the transparent eagle of evening wouldn't get us
and the hum of adults from the street
and the sea, the sea, which threatened (protected?)
that fino del primo tempo.

It was forever summer, a light summer
a summer of water and sandals, immune
to that alcohol, soon to be called Love,
—and in the deserted pavilion (in vain you'd look for it.
It's either been removed with two fingers
from its ring of earth by War, or by some
useful work, or else forgotten).
We were playing childhood, but, in fact,
I can't remember anyone, I don't think
there was another child apart from me,
because, see, I can only remember
a lonely flight into mystery
staged by the gestures of the sea, I remember
only the happiness, oh God, of leaning
with bare arms and legs on warm stones,
of sloping ground, with grass,
of the innocent air of evening.

Flowers smelt dizzily in that place
where, a little above men and women,
who definitely smelt of tobacco
hot barbecue and beer, I
was running, unaware of my ugly head,
breaking, in fact, the soft head from the flower
and kissing it on the lips
While the sea also smelt more strongly
than now, it was wilder, its seaweed
darker, and cursed the rocks
even more in the way it whipped them.
It wasn't far from home
to that place, I could run there
and back and no one would miss me,
in four steps and eight jumps I was there,
but, first, I stole from fences
feathers of peacocks left between slats,
most beautiful feathers, I've not seen since
with the immense blue green eye
and with golden eyelashes so long
that I was holding a whole bird in my hands
not part of one
and I was tearing at feathers
stuck between the slats
tearing at something from the mystery
of those fiendish courtyards
and then I was running towards the deserted pavilion
from the edge of the sea
and I was running round it and through it
through derelict rooms
where mad martins battered themselves against walls,
with the ceiling bursting outside and in, as if within me.

I wore a short sleeveless dress
the colour of sand when sun runs out of strength
and in the autumn I should have gone to school,
and the performance of the sea kept breaking my rib cage

to make me more roomy, that's why
my heart was beating and even now the cage in my
chest hurts
at the memory of that beat of the sea
while attempting to enter me
especially at evening when flowers fade
without losing their colour completely,
staying pink with tea, violet with milk,
losing only their stems in the darkness,
floating, beheaded, at a certain height
above the grass which had also vanished.
This is a tremendous memory,
absolutely unforgettable,
the feeling of a light, unchained body,
invulnerable, perfect, my head,
just a natural extension of it.
Supervising only its speed and orientation.
Yet I never hurt myself,
I can't remember ever having fallen that summer.
I was light, extremely healthy,
inspired, and if I wasn't flying
it was only because I preferred to run on earth
and not for any other reason.

And after that . . .
What was I saying? Ah, yes, I had long bare legs
and bare slender arms
and in the deserted pavilion there was this strange
coolness
as if an invisible sea had breezed through it . . .

And after that . . .
—Where was I? Ah, yes, the flowers full of night . . .
like sacred smoke
and my lonely flight
through gentle and benevolent mysteries . . .

And after that? . . .

LONGING

My lover,
heavy anchor,
holds me tight:
everything's hurting,
mouth—from longing,
eyes—from crying.

winds have dropped—
well—maybe not,
but it was growing
calmer in the sky,
powerless
as in the beginning.

I don't dream now
of steps in snow,
of foxes' traces
no more flowers
their souls
sleep in bulbs.

Loneliness . . .
My search pointless—
you—intangible.
No news of you.
How real are you?
How real were you?

*　*　*

The kitten doesn't spare the mother
because of her severed tail.

It keeps on biting the still bleeding stump:
the mother cat meeows pitifully
trying to push him away gently with her paw
but the kitten doesn't give up,
bites, tiny bites—
the stump of a tail
got by the zest of kids in the street:
tight tying of wire
(sometime ago
when the cat was still pregnant).

*   *   *

In a solar grand old age
cheerful flies pester me
because I smell of honey and sea.
I bury myself gradually and greedily.
My sumptuous greenish hair
protects me from the looks
of the few aggressors
coming from the sea
on long ships lacquered with blood.

In the shelter of my age
I hear my nails growing.

DENISA COMANESCU was born in Buzău in 1954. She studied Romanian and English at Bucharest University. The first of her three volumes of verse received the Debut prize of the Writers' Union in 1979. She works at present for the *Universe Publishing House*.

FAMILY PORTRAIT

Again Dad's left the washing from the laundry
on a market stall
my sister writes herself
love letters
to show me triumphantly.
Mum pays for prayers given secretly
(Please God give my girls
the happiness you never gave me.)
While writing on the balcony on my knees
a little frog enters the house
quite unperturbed
and I've none to share
the delight of this sight with—
for you
were dedicated to death.

BANISHMENT FROM
PARADISE 1979

I'm up to here with you—
he shouted
and wanted to kick me out there and then
from the apartment
I'd not paid a penny for
all that time
every day three girls
came knocking at the door:
one had an exotic name
and one was obsessed with the occult
the last led a pure but fine life.
But where to go
my youth hides behind rubbish bins
where even gypsies no longer rummage
and poetry is declared a forbidden zone
where the law of Malthus is strictly applied.
Go to the park, he said
just as the watchman at the cemetery had mumbled
when hand in hand I'd walked
with my first boy friend:
'The park's the place for making love!'

*   *   *

It's nightime and it's raining
through the drab air
I travel
along a deserted highway

on a large swan
no lantern shines
nerves prick
every particle of air ten times
ready to catch
any wave
approaching
from a new paradise:
my excited brain's a mouse-trap.

X-RAY

She broke into the apartment
and smashed all my records
(pride and joy of 15 years)
She threw my books out of the window
demanding
(and she wasn't joking
she even said that sooner or later
they'd come to shake you up a bit)
to see my soul.
In vain I explained that my life
was nothing but a Grecian profile
she insisted on not hearing
God knows what cry
wild beast's or baby's
'cos she didn't sense the swan's despair
when the earth devours the stream.
Then bored
she handed me some paper
where a rotten pressed rose lay:
—I haven't got the soul you want
instead
from under the counter
someone sold me
an X-ray of one just like it:
take it
and perhaps
by morning it'll bloom.

MEETING A PLAY BOY

In me the hardworking ant of chance has found a
                                    reliable warehouse
one more golden rain
once more a limp body electrified
like a cat before a bird
I look into the mirror
my face seems unfamiliar: too radiant
too triumphant (as though by washing my hair
with a yolk it's be thick by morning)
how can I make him realize, or understand
that it's just a balloon I cover with care
so as not to get pricked by pointed objects everywhere?
That I won't have enough hands, or tits, or lips
to save it.
Play-boy, Play-boy, take pity on this woman
who can't re-invent love except through your love

ROBINCRUSADE

I stay clinging to the room
killing sentiments
by ironing.
As I would flies.
But this feeling grips me
like a corset.
I feel like the boiler
the coffee-grinder
the paraffin can
the bulldozer
the very delicate nightdress.
Oh if only I were a ship
my love would make sure
I had a perfect sea
the gentlest swell
and a miraculous island
of people.

EARTH

Such a still
night
like death.
I keep vigil
like an open
coffin.
After the last nail
hammered in the morning
take care
not to tread too heavily
when you walk
on me.

TO THE FRIEND WHO ASKED ME
TO DEDICATE THIS POEM TO V

There's no seed of victory planted in me.
Some plants that take root
in a glass of water
vigorous like some Jesuit
they forage into rocks
decapitate towns
move Heaven and Hell.
Oh, volcanic temperaments,
I've licked so much ash
until the sun rose
in my womb
but since then I shine
shine.

IOANA CRACIUNESCU is an actress by profession. She was born in November 1950 and studied at the Institute of Dramatic Art in Bucharest, joining the Nottara Theatre Company in 1973. She has written five volumes of verse and was awarded the Bucharest Writers' Union Prize in 1981.

Iona Crǎciunescu

CLINICAL WINTER

I'm frightened and ashamed
of myself, of my bones, of my sex.

There exists a return to growth,
a rearranging of death in tissue,
a happiness of depravation.

A sledge like a roller, pulled by reindeer,
gets into your bed, sites itself on your chest with all its
weight,
Looks you in the eye, spits images of childhood in your
face,
—little bells, harshness deafening you—it's snowing
in your brain.

Where have all your views vanished to
all your doggy friends
with their fawning, their courteous growling . . .

In the alleys near the madhouse white pigeons peck
grains
snow
my nerves, barracks of soldiers:– always on the alert.

In night's memory
your image springs—ferocious, agile as a panther!

Iona Crăciunescu

INVOLUNTARY MEMORY

Now—
in a pub some drunkards accost you
with lewd gestures
their words piercing right into you fresh
from the sewers.
they shower you, splash you, and there's no protection.

Soon even your words come out smelling
of cabbage and drink.

You envy the comfort of the one who wakes
with a loaded tongue and he knows that this is a certain
sign of disease.

The impossibility of you poking out your tongue
yellow and acrid as a medal!

And just then, suddenly, there springs to mind for the
first time
the honest advice of the crippled grandfather
given on your third birthday:
Don't cry on the shoulder of a statue!
Don't look for support on the prop of a vine!
Don't wet your bed!
Eat up everything on your plate, wipe your mouth
with your ambitions! I'm past it!
But you're destined for a great failure!

Iona Crăciunescu

PEACOCKS IN THE OLD PARK

Try to put up with your failure.
I think your logic's worthless!

In the hesitation of the flesh Spring has burst out.
You can feel yourself running in the green meadow
and you're not ashamed that you resemble goat and kid.

You make love with the peacocks in the old park,
the brick in the walls crack from your heat.

You can say nothing to the one who watches you from
the shadows,
To the one who undresses you with lucid eyes,
You can say nothing!
You make shrill noises and the pairing you deny
illuminates you!

What you want can no longer be, but
did you ever really know what you wanted?

You stay stretched out in the green meadow,
a herd of lambs graze madly from your flesh.

Iona Crăciunescu

RHETORIC

Oh
you
animal of a disappearing species
protected by the law
with sealed fodder
with pumped gurgling water,
don't you feel the need (my kin)
to throw yourself onto the barbed wire surrounding
the woods?

IN THE DARK

I was groping in the dark.
Luminous gut! —and I couldn't find his bones
and I couldn't find his soul
and I couldn't find his heart.

What a fountain of murkiness, what slow hurried
goodness:

I was moulding you from air you were breathing
Seeing you as both subject and king
in a palace of hopeless carressing

you were the backbone of my brain

darling.

Iona Crăciunescu

MY ATTENTION WANDERS

You were (still) showing your son
how to use a compass
while I separated my muscles from the bones
with the skill of a starved fish-eater.

(In a sack, in a paltry rubbish bin
wrapped in newspaper, left on the street—
that white flesh.)

You were (still) digesting the family meal
while I crawled through empty museums
recreating famous paintings with the shadows of the
                                            lights.

Sun, so much sun outside!

Plaster busts on shelves, shining. Books and mouldings.
Love stories digesting their identity in golden
lenses. Surgery needles tenderly sewing tapestry.
My attention wanders!

(I'm a sack, in a paltry rubbish bin
wrapped in newspaper, left on the street—
that white flesh.)

WITH BLOUSE UNDONE

He spotted me, blouse undone, through the crack of the
door

sweating
I was helping the bitter cherries in the furniture to
flourish

with blouse undone and no strength left in my voice

Iona Crăciunescu

RED FOXES WITH NIGHT-LOVE RINGS UNDER THEIR EYES

Can the armour cross the square,
unlock the gate, climb to the attic,
to sleep without the one who wears it?

and then somewhat later
    (Many manoeuvres—many sieges later)

see the loved one disarmed, descending
in the mirror.

Just us swimming in black silver
young insomnias—eyes shining.

ITINERARY

You can't find the promised city anywhere!

You pay to visit churches,
Evaluated faith—clock of the planets.

Grouse squeal in the suitcase of clothes
a mother's death rattle in a golden manger

the favourite, the winner, the lover,
practises flying above the precipice of flesh

and falls
falls

falls.

JEWEL OF THE COLD

How you settle on me like frost
(the feet of night freeze me)
your embrace a jewel of the cold
you tread on me on hazel bows
over the abyss of my nature.

You leave me like ashes spread on icy roads
(just as last winter you left a blanket of quinces
in the cemetery's frozen grounds).

You implant knives into lemon buds all
acrid from thirst,
I decipher your closeness, like a Japanese sign
grief stricken on the wall.

THURSDAY

Maybe in the afternoon
I'll dress in silky brown
when I climb high to see the town
and so look beautiful
to throw myself down.

DANIELA CRASNARU was born in Craiova in 1950. She studied
Romanian and English at Craiova University, graduating in
1973, the year in which her first volume of poetry was
published. To date she has written eight volumes and a
number of children's books. She has won a poetry prize of
the Writer's Union and at present is an editor with the
Eminescu Publishing House.

THE THIRTY YEAR OLD BODY

I've stopped fighting you,
neurotic cage.
I've raised the drawbridge,
banished my ambassadors.
Vainly you send bored messengers,
salesmen of illusions.
All sales are over.
Nothing's left but a small incandescent crystal
which anyway's the lion's share.
And the lion himself will come. Very soon.
But his majestic grip
won't even honour you by crushing you.
Thirty years, my fears
like a legion of blinds
over your dizzy thresholds.
Thirty years, my spirit
a corporal marching over your glorious remains
carrying a kitbag of words on its back.
that's the end of it. Your shameless luck,
your shining misery
won't hear from me
another word.
Thirty years I've polished them,
those bars, now ending loving them
while increasing them.

ONTO THE STRAIGHT

Words above facts
words like huge Saint-Bernards
warming the victims with their own bodies,
every now and again saving what's left to be saved.
With more and more difficulty my memory traverses
the dark canals, abattoirs of terror,
where corpses hover over
some earlier cheers.
The snow-covered bell of a Christmas card,
hundreds of hands jostling to ring it.
Yet stubbornly it remains mute and heavenly
purely an aesthetic object, there, in the reality
of a card from childhood.
The last turning and then onto the straight.
By now my mind should be clear, clear; the order of its
                                    corridors—perfect.

Last efforts calculated with precision.
Last love, last honoured duty;
the last word, a Saint-Bernard, crouching over me
with its chest fiery, fiery, fiery.

THE STAGE DRESSING ROOM

To watch the performance
as if not one image could prey
on the peace of your docile retina.
To remain in semi-darkness of illusion, alone.
Your small kingdom, the stage dressing room.
King Lear throws his crown away
hurriedly donning Phaedra's gown.
Medea searches the subtext anxiously.
In five lines, in two,
who was to be killed is killed
who was to be deceived is deceived.
Innocence enters self-assured in the cloak of a henchman.
Happiness in the cloak of an indolent old man.
Only the hopeless haven't time to don
another disguise
five lines, two, —now!
Dark, props, trunks, cauldrons, chairs—a broken one,
you can't find the door to the stage
but find yourself on the service stairs
which anyway lead you out.
In the middle of the crowd waiting for standing room
          only,
suddenly a respectful space is made:
arriving, now at the last moment, the car of the leading
          comedian.
Hurrying, for he must appear on stage.
He can't accept that he of all people,
can be paid for nothing, he, the one who knows all the
          parts,
grocer, porter, nanny, Roman emperor, cobbler,
first soldier, second soldier, great inquisitor,
gentle pontiff, people, crowd.

He enters quickly, cloakroom attendants simper with
                                        delight,
the make-up girl sighs discreetly,
the wig-maker and stage hand bow, smiling with
                                        admiration.
One line, two, five. Just the same . . .
Who was to be killed was killed,
what was promised was promised, who was to be
                                kissed was kissed.
The son, Hippolytus, smiles knowingly.
For ages Polonius gnaws the curtain.
How much longer? seems to be the question,
until a voice, obviously off stage,
from outside your dressing-room
says to you, and only to you:
just near here is an arena.
Sweepers fly happily through its dust.
Very soon the gladiators will prepare
a finale no less than out of this world.
But we don't have a lion that's good enough, a tiger
                                or some
feline to put everything she's got into it.
Wouldn't you like to have a go, you who are, if you'll
                                excuse the liberty,
just the actor's understudy?
Perhaps a jump, and if possible a bend, just naturally,
a jolly good lion's snarl. And
(if we're not by any chance taking an advantage . . .)
                                a scream
towards the end. But with lots of feeling.

TRANSYLVANIAN TOWN

Do you remember the town where we once went
                                    together?
Delirious streets climbing higher,
keyboards of a piano, a sonorous stair.
It happened an eternity ago. Now an era, a year.

It was a mediaeval town, walled and scholastic.
Climbing of our own free will, two heretics
on a huge stake.
Two handsome heretics, swimming through waters of
                                    dusk
through time stopped at the town's gate.

The clock in the tower had no hands, no hours.
Sweet fragrance drifting over everything, oh such
                                    aromas.
Do you remember how our bodies and breath drew
                                    signs
On the white pages of calendars?

We were there in a time without a name.
Always near evening, almost never near daytime.
It's a year now since we were there, a decade.
Another millenium. Another lifetime.

AGELESS DIALOGUE

Poetry, sad luxury,
cynical century when many
on earth wonder why
poets don't ever walk barefoot.
To make concrete contact with the ground.
So I found.
Contractors ensure
points never rust.
Before the eyes,
your daily bread is greater than a planet.
For this sky that's free
a mortal obeisance,
a pirouette.
The naive wonder, clowns ponder,
the man of genius debates upon
why the century of enlightenment
didn't last at least a millenium?
What are you doing in there?
Under the pyramid of hollow gestures,
and words?
Look I still breathe,
(Loud cheers).

TELEX

Top Hat factory on strike. Destruction.
Vatican, Holy scriptures learned from compendium.

Mortality courses by correspondence. Successes.
Statue of Liberty more military crosses.

New illness discovered. Volunteers recruiting.
Watchmen and Porters—refresher training.

Chance tries in vain to follow moral code
Orpheus—last vocal chord, sold.

THE REHEARSAL STUDIO

The rehearsal studio. Cool. Semi-darkness.
We start again. We polish the scene.
The same scene.
Its shadowy corpse
abandoned under flocks of devouring words.
Once again, calls the director,
take it from the loathing. No, from affection,
from doubt.
Now lunge, hold it, breathe!
Get closer to the chalk lines
that centre, the core,
from which only the right gestures can stream, will
                                    stream out,
only the sincere attitudes we all need
so much.
Of course the right's yours to choose between pirouette
and curtsey, between kneeling
and crawling, breakdown and flight.
But please be a bit more natural!
For Christ's sake can't you imagine
that here is the water, and there's the woods.
that it won't be long now, only three lines
before a saving hand will pull you up by the hair
to finally get you out
of this endless whirlpool.
Close your eyes like this . . .
Imagine that the wind's blowing gently, gently,
that you're at home and that you're ten years old,
your mother and father are alive,
extremely young and gay
and only then say that key line
the one that holds up the whole scaffolding,
the whole classical scene of that classical text

which in no way can be changed
by lighting, scenery or direction.
There's no choice here. Do you get my meaning?
If so, let's get on.
From the desperation. No from confusion. No
from the beginning.

EVERYTHING IS FOR OUR OWN GOOD

Everything is for our own good.
Road sweepers who stop us falling
on banana skins.
The card you clock in with.
The heavenly view of the park in autumn.
The anadin, the valium, the ethic and rhetoric.
The hotel receptionist, who carefully checks
that we don't have different names (Wink! Wink!)
that we don't have different addresses (Nudge! Nudge!)
                              the laws, decrees,
and their amendments.
Everything is for our own good.
The (ancient) inscriptions HIC FUIT . . .
and the (modern) imperatives: don't walk on the grass,
don't slam the door, don't leave me yet. Don't . . .
                              purely and simply
carefully and gently with our lives
so that in no way can we go off the rails,
when
everything is for our own good:
the (verbal) reprimand of friends
the (written) reprimand of public opinion
the increased salary, services of small cooperatives
messengers of love, the agony columns.
Hearts, lungs and brain.
God, how ashamed I've become.
Everything's for our own good.
Benevolent Funds and X rays,
blood from the O Group,
and radium, radium, radium.

Daniela Crăsnaru

EXTREMELY FEMININE

(Oh, you, sentiments so heretical and pathetic
And, you, attitudes so ironical and Platonic)

Everything's as I said, just like the Book,
I'm an incorrigible optimist, like sleepwalkers
on the edge of a roof—floating.
The grip of an absurd calm, rooted in death,
cures me daily of any longing.

In the air hours plough walls and tunnels,
lilies poke out their tongues at me, shamelessly.
My skin that's suffering, or only missing
makes wrinkles, passionately.

Blood breaks hidden shutters
in an unknown, nameless deep.
'Perhaps tomorrow I'll not eat you either,' the bored
                                          wolf says,
who comes at night to my sleep.

No one subjects me to force
or threatens me with force
even less with love or tenderness.
Only the claw of the moment leers lustily
for the vein in my neck.

I make obeisance and pirouette,
I pay threefold and, finally,
to keep balance and planetary calm
I tell you daily
I'm fine.

Daniela Crăsnaru

SYNCHRONISM
TWENTIETH CENTURY

While you say 'Good evening' to me, caressing my brow:

—The company which for two thousand years has handled
    the hammering of nails strictly in those places described
    in that well-known classical myth,
    is daily looking for a cheaper material than iron,
    more pliable, more efficient (yet of course never
    for a moment turning the conveyor belt off).

—In a sterile room two pipettes kiss frantically:
    retorts, computers, clink-clink-clink
    reveal the place of the 'miracle' reaction:
    there in the liquid of the test-tube, cloudy
    like the sand of some prehistoric sea
    is constructed from atoms and seconds
    the mystery of creation.

—A hurricane with an exotic name, a coastal warning sign,
    a train full of hopes
    cross the heart, the mind, the soul
    on that divine artery.
    During this time
    I'm checking pearls for quality control.
    You know, the same ones, those domestic creatures
    who could only be there in that Latin language.

Daniela Crăsnaru

THE ART OF KNOCKING
THE NAIL ON THE HEAD

In the reassuring half-light
her eyes see the event
as from another planet (Heh,
you wretched reed, flattened to the earth
the fiery earth,
Monsieur Pascal—what does he know!):

flurried hands of the male
with the haste of a soldier
the flittering shadow of clothes
thrown to the floor in a heap
the watch placed nearby.

A slight wave of nausea
a Sunday from adolescence
with servant girls hanging around
the green fence of the barracks

a slight wave of chill
from head to toe
from head to toe shaken
by the arguments of this man
rapidly and precisely given
with one eye on the clock
arguments with no right of appeal
inescapable axioms
which despite all her efforts,
reasoning
tells her—don't quite ring true.

CAROLINA ILICA was born in March 1951 in the village of Viedra. She graduated in Philosophy and in 1965 she made her poetic debut in the Review *Flacâra Roşie*. Her first volumes of poetry appeared in 1974 followed by others in 1975 and 1977. Recently two volumes with the same title appeared, one of which was in poetic prose. Among her translations is a volume of Armenian poetry.

SO TIRED

I'm almost tired enough to drop
from something sad, that can't be said;
a whirlpool, of which I'm the prop,
has wrapped me round, from foot to head.

I'm like a fruit that's dropping low
towards the grass rough with rye.
on bedding with a dusky glow;
I'm almost ripe enough to die.

(translated by Fleur Adcock)

Carolina Ilica

THE NIGHT PLANE

Autumn peaches smelling, brutally, small
  Small, with red core, bitter-sweet
    Bitter which you chew
      You chew after bitter pills
        After very bitter pills

        Remedy against the sickness called
        Bitterness (and more gravely:
        Becoming insane)

While above the town rasps
Yet another plane

Carolina Ilica

THE CRY OF LIFE

Aged is the face of the rose;
    tired petals,
    tired eyelids.
(In parks the month of autumn catches
    the rose's
    suicide.)

How heavy will be the sleep of those
    comforted
    by no one!
And how late will
    the guilty
    keep vigil!

But after the grip of pain what
    maternal
    gentleness
    the tired woman
    breathes—
When the cry of life
    has cut
    like lightning.

MINE ALONE

I don't hide anything because nothing can be hidden.

The smile and the eyes and the hands
are unashamedly
exposed to sight.
The cloak takes the shape of the tall body,
the sandal shows off the leg.

Pains from inside call out my name
the heart
most often.

What about Thought?
    I hear you say.

It's always got
favourite traitors: A gesture,
                a Word,
                    a Dream.

And yet I feel something's mine alone:
A Museum of Memories: a unique collection,
which no one could ever crowd
into the frame of memory.

THE RAIN ON THE WINDOW

I am a Pisces; I like water. Rain liberates me, gives me that euphoric state of purity; not a primary purity but one which I could name; fruit of purgatory.

Down, on the leaves, on the grass, on the pavement, herds of rain canter with hooves; before my eyes the open window, the manes of drops, through which you can just make out a scene from the house opposite:

Under the bed of a child: a big bird;
It lifts him rocking from one wing to another.

I stare: it's an angel

NIGHT'S ATTRACTION

How can I rely on you?!
You more woman than I, promising so much
                              yet giving nothing!
you rock me in sleep, kiss me all over,
Impudent one!
And you force me to dream your way and to wonder:

> —How well it suits
>   your white body
>   with blonde hair to be
>   in my arms more black
>   than blackness!

But how hurried you were this morning—today at dawn!
How could those frighten you:

> a child
> deflowering her hearing
> with her own shrieking!

INCITAMENTUM MUSICA SENSUM

Opposite the block where I live, as you'd expect
there's another; I leave the window open—

> because it's summer
> and because I like the music
> coming from the other side;
> it's as old as a memory
> and just as unsettling.

The books,
  flowers,
    my clothes

are silent:
and obediently stay in their place!

> Only children aren't obedient:
> or pious; but full of impatience.
> Oh, look slipping away towards me
> from a framed picture,
> comes your childhood face!
> lips growing, running,
> (they've reached me; they kiss me)—
> your lips!

ILEANA MALANCIOIU was born in January 1940 in the county
of Argeş. She received a first degree in Philosophy from
Bucharest University in 1968 and completed her doctorate in
the same discipline seven years later. She has worked for
Romanian television and the literary review *Argeş* and is at
present an editor with the literary monthly *Viaţa Românească*.
One of the most prolific of contemporary Romanian poets,
Ileana produced her first volume in 1967 and since then has
published nine collections of verse. She was awarded the
Poetry Prize of the Writers' Union in 1979.

ALONE IN A DARK THEATRE

Alone in a dark theatre
The great performance is for me alone
All the Stars of the world are on stage
But now their light can no longer shine.

I've no idea who's stopped it
And I don't know why or for how long
In the empty theatre where I stand
You can hear the stars' sad song.

Don't shout, they told me, or they'll be panic
Things must be taken as they're found
So I don't shout or try to run
But quietly sink into the ground.

UP TO THE LIMIT

The only human feeling was fear
And just then we'd become soft-hearted
That's why we gathered more often,
And like parrots, words were repeated.

This same thing was made to tear apart
That peace we'd always striven for
Of which we thought again and again as it went
Once and for all.

We talked together about better times
But in the silence in which we were waiting
I couldn't even open my mouth
For fear was the only human feeling.

LAST MEMORY

I stood face to face with the inventor
Of the fear I felt each morning
And I froze as I looked into his eyes
And they were trembling.

Like two canals
Through which emptiness flows
Towards this world
As liquid goes

Through a U-tube
I stood face to face with the inventor
And from his large eyes
Sprang corpses as if from the centre

Of the well of our death to come
And I was thinking how to stretch my hand
Towards those canals of emptiness
To end this stress.

LOVE STORY

Everything began with great enthusiasm
I would have died without you, you without me
When suddenly we both died I don't know how
And on a day so frantically busy.

We were having the meal at the usual time
And no one else noticed it
Friends danced awhile and then left
The blaring tape played on for a bit

Sounding happier than anyone else
Then unexpectedly everything ended
And we stayed together just out of habit
In neighbouring graves, just like the dead.

SERENITY

Yet another man carries his cross on his back
Serene as though he carried a sack to the mill
We all watch him as he enters the cemetery
And nobody's spine feels a sudden chill

That he's written his own name on the stone
And will mark the green earth with it
Only just paid for as though he were afraid
That otherwise he'd lose it

Despite the fact that he seems so certain.
Yet another man makes his way over there
Completely at peace carrying the cross
That his whole life has taught him to bear.

SHE WAS DRESSED LIKE ME

She was dressed like me
And even had powder on
Only she was smiling
And lying down

In the middle of the crowd
And didn't know
How many people had come to her
From everywhere.

She was dressed like me
And we even seemed to have the same nature
And we even looked similar
And yet how different we were.

TWO FRIENDS

It's snowing, once more the traces
Of this very sad winter are covered;
It's snowing over those who've passed as though
They ought never to have existed.

I want to get out of here, who knows
How many more winters I might be seeing
I'm taking this cemetery on my back
It's still snowing there and I'm leaving.

Two friends call to me softly from the snows.
Our dear friend, you'll never be able to carry us
No one's going to allow you more
Than a cross.

THIS WINTER TOO WILL PASS

This winter too will pass, it's bound to.
That's what I was thinking in bed today at noon
I was neither too hot nor too cold
I didn't know whether I'd only just laid down

Or whether I'd slept and a day had gone by
I was in that nightdress I'd started to wear
Day and night, I was in a dream
I was in your soul, that of a dead man

Which I'd entered a few seconds before.
I avoided if fearfully
Just as I would this frozen room
And was glad it wasn't empty

Or at least that's how it seemed
Although I could see nothing odd
Even if you no longer knew the reality
I was glad it wasn't sad.

ANTIGONE

A frozen hill, white body of a dead man
left above the world fallen in heavy battle
hungry dogs come and bite the treacherous snow
and another winter comes to take a bite as well.

Let a virgin appear, to break the command
to wrench that fantastic hill from the dogs
and hide it like a dear brother
while those closest to her wash their hands of it

and they'll let her be buried alive in the earth
clothed in this unreal white
for while the emperor lost that great battle
she wept and buried a hill

CONFUSION

I didn't know what I was doing. I'd forgotten everything
Like a sleepwalker on your roof, I was climbing
and no one dared to stop my progress
and I kept disturbing

your sleep, and finally I woke you
and brought you in a frenzy
this new harvest of spring
which could have filled a great cemetery

ANGELA MARINESCU was born in 1941. She studied medicine at Cluj University and went on to complete a degree in Psychology at Bucharest University in 1971. She has published six volumes of verse to date. In 1980 she took the unusual step of refusing the Writers' Union prize for her volume *Structura Nopții*.

* * *

Small crystals of honey settling
over the kindled pupils of my eyes
erode the revered tiny stems
and other small structures which bleed
into every moment.
Through the cold mists of darkness
comes a blind woman unknown to me
thrusting her knife blade into blackness

Angela Marinescu

* * *

A strong black
hand
clenched
over the brain
dagger into dagger:
bitter as void.

Angela Marinescu

* * *

To caress the wound (the brain) with the mouth

those nailed breathe the narrow air
the leaves, like cells, drip outwards
you want the trace of blood lost
the dead victim—white

in the moment of fusion the sane one loses his mind
pure blood
concise memory of death—
a mask.

* * *

The dream. Collapse into water. In thought
you return to the placenta.
The tearing of dignity like the limp net
brought to shore, crafty, cunning, a naked devil.
That's how it ought to have been. There are things
which I can tell only to myself.
Before me like a despairing universe echoes
the wave which has but one law.
There are things which none can stop,
nor erase. When I realized, it was as though
I'd put my hand into the fire.
Loneliness is ash.
Nothing can make it anything else.
Nothing can prevent its coming.
It should neither chain nor extol you.
The child you bore from nothing,
death which comes from nothing.
From what shouldn't have been
from an existence you never asked for, full of matter,
dense, brutal, formless with no chance of cover.
Not even a word can be covered.
The fanaticism of love resembles the seed of blood in
                                        every
word.
If I could be covered in words,
in words
of sun. SUN.

Angela Marinescu

*   *   *

A dense crowd, tired, stays gathered
round smokey tables in translucent houses
cells of non-being! My cell
is cold and black.
My loneliness is matter, an object,
brutal, violent,
to be shot at,
to be avoided.

Angela Marinescu

*   *   *

I slide past stealthily, my harshness that of precision.
It's known what I can do,
how far I can go
towards evil, towards the roots of evil,
to the essence of evil, beyond evil,
shaking my being, shaking that compact sanctity—

the spinal column bathed in blood.

Angela Marinescu

I'm just the tree
at the side of the road
no lonelier or more powerful
but nevertheless
devastated by darkness.

So much disgust and so much shadow
I transform my blood into an
object or a being
with soul and flesh,
but the one abandoned by love, just like me,
will meet a violent death.

GRETE TARTLER was born in Bucharest in 1948. She studied at the Ciprian Porumbescu Conservatory from which she graduated in 1972. While a teacher of the viola at a secondary school, she enrolled at Bucharest University to study Arabic and English. She obtained her degree in 1976 by which time she had already published two volumes of verse. Four further volumes followed and in 1978 she was awarded the Poetry Prize of the Writers' Union. She has also translated extensively from classical Arabic literature.

IDENTIFICATION SIGN

I'm skinning a fruit, this blood-red scalp,
I'm leafing through a medieval torture manual—
judges are condemning to death without trial,
the one left without friends is knocked to the ground,
and his blood sucked dry.
The loud rattling of keys is heard on the corridor,
the late shift slams the door of the lift
left open by those from the earlier shift;
Now would be the time to throw away
the poems written in the summer
kept with the thought of rewriting them sometime—
but it's not too bad to keep old stuff in cupboards
if this is the price for having faith in the future.
Now would be the time
to retreat like the wise to the wilderness.
I can hear the telly on next door,
the whistling of the wind, the identification sign
of a friend from another life.
Hand on the door handle I take the pulse of the house,
and wait close beside it:
just like the one who catches snakes
but knows that one night he'll be bitten.

THE TROUT

(To the music of Schubert)

From the town, the poet leaves for the woods,
towards glittering waterfalls.
He has a small spear; at home,
a plentiful supply of glowing coals.
'I'm going to catch you, sly deceiver,
then impale you with a procedure
seen in Arab manuals of torture
I'll lie you on the coals, skin you alive
But before all
this,
whether or not there's anyone else in the woods,
I'm going to make you scream!
Just to prove you've got a voice.'

TROUBADOUR

It's not to the first love I should be singing,
but to the last, the one that leads to dying.
PLACE AND DATE OF BIRTH: Bucharest November 23rd.

Romanian.

Love—poison from a felled maple.
A cry between two armies in battle.
EDUCATION: Romance, classical, oriental languages. Violin.
Love that makes even the coward brave,
And keeps my sleepy spirit alive.
COLOUR OF EYES: Brown. DISTINGUISHING FEATURES: None.
Love which at the start was fun in a name
But, butterfly, you fell in the flame.
CRIMINAL RECORD: None.
Love—magnet of blood and bone,
a prison eternally pressing you down.
OCCUPATION: Twentieth Century. Anon.

FIRST SNOW

The teacher gathers in the worksheets:
1. What is good?   2. What is bad?
3. What is hard?   3. What is simple?

Good is liberty. Life. Peaches and cream.
Something clean. Helping a friend.
Good is living as well as you can.

Bad is breaking windows. Tripping someone up.
Not to live. War. Forgetting.
Throwing stones. Putting your life in danger.

Hard is to tell the truth. A metal bar.
A body in space. To live in terror.
To be alone.

Simple is a grain of wheat. To do what you like.
The air. A feather. To play.
To believe a lie.

'I'd have been better asking
The colour of the first snow,' thinks the teacher.
The pupils murmur. Whisper in each others' ears.
A girl begins to cry.

DIDACTICA NOVA

How many fingers have you got on one hand?
Five, replied the child.
So, how many do five and five make?
Eleven, comes the answer.
Can you blame me for getting cross with you?
Didn't I say count?
Why can't you understand
And answer like all the rest!
What if everyone answered like that?
What would happen if nobody understood?
How many fingers have you got on one hand?
Five, replied the child.
Well, how many on two hands?
Eleven comes the answer.
The blows fall. On the hand with five fingers,
On the hand
    with six.

PLAYBACK

'I love you,' you tell me, but who's saying it for you?
It's just like that day in Cairo—
I heard cries of Crusaders
Coming from a crowded coach of tourists—
And instead of my voice
The whistling of an arrow.
'I love you,' you tell me,
The voice of the actor hired
To say it all for you
In a foreign language.

THE GODDESS OF FASHION

Dior gives names to haute couture
Albert Camus, Marcel Ayme, Jean-Paul Sartre.
For your sake. I could almost wear
A cape of snow
Which one day would bear
Your name.
As on a peacock's tail
And my many, brown, wide open eyes
Would pass quickly through your body
Like mice through an icy winter.

THE STRAIGHT LINE

You're picking the stalk of a sunflower
from between the railway sleepers:
'After thousands of miles you think of returning.'
The yellow river is flowing too slowly—
the clay of the world, the words
follow a straight line, as they leave town.
If you see poetry as an old railwayman does
and still think the last word's
yet to be said
if the train's whistle is enough for you
(the certainty being: 'I resound')
if you still think they'll unmask themselves
to meet the poet in you
and you're not afraid that you'll hit your head
because you were too shortsighted to see the sleeper,
then follow the straight line,
as you leave town

A WHITE CORRIDOR

A column of ants passing through a clean
skull, in deep green grass:
perhaps it's the very bull who recently
grazed this plain.

I watch them—and drag you behind me through
the whitest of corridors, the skull of a god:
for a moment in the dry eye sockets we taste the heavenly
nectar, that's only just vanished.

Grete Tartler

LOVE POEM

In my left eyelid strikes a figureless clock,
poems are struck by the typewriter, slaves with a whip.
Speak up now, Novalis, you engineer of mines,
of labyrinths you can't escape from with just a spun thread,
how can you hear the voiceless call, the truth-lie in words?
Maybe tonight you're lying down,
while I stand in fullness of day:
our shadows form a cross.
Someone strikes home the nails. Perhaps there is time
to endure this rumble, the struck metal,
the snaking heat that blackens our faces,
perhaps there's time for us to remember being born,
for me to bathe in your eyes the colour of amniotic waters
for us to be thrilled by youth and hailstones
(if these are our finest years, God help them!)
Perhaps there's time to get ready for parties
where invited guests never arrive, to repeat
to the child the advice of our mothers,
to forget what we've learned, to travel
together to the Orient, to listen
to rowdy neighbours through pipes in the wall,
perhaps there's time for essentials and trifles,
but then again
perhaps there isn't time.

DOINA URICARIU was born in October 1950. She studied
French and Romanian at Bucharest University and now
works as an editor for the *Eminescu Publishing House*. Her
publications include five volumes of verse and critical studies
of the Romanian poet Emil Botta.

Doina Uricariu

MADONNA AND THE PLOUGHSHARE

Barbaric bliss,
nothing's taken from your bitter slice.
Like uncut pages in a volume of silk—so beautiful
and yet like so many things—doubtful.

I'm supporting all round
the skin of a child filled with whispering
and this breast that keeps on growing
under the milky spring.

SMALL SPLINTERS
FROM MY CHEEK

Happiness blood from my blood.

Sometimes truth keeps quiet
pretending to be something else:
I talk about the claws of a bird,
they scratch into my shoulder,
But this strange tale describes
the time just after feeding,
tender, ferocious, domestic,
hair done up in plaits,
the small body has turned its back
and serenely submerges into me.

Happiness usurps and steals.
Small splinters from my cheek hit me.

THE HELMSMAN OF PAIN

Who's going to benefit from the work?
From the legislator?
The soul's shuttle weaves its thin cloak,
a shroud is the only consolation,
ten fingers across the body
know the answer better than any other oracle,
just as the stone will always reach its target
and the fire is always lit.

On the neck the sign of death is a perfect flower,
just as love is a perfect wound
and again I see that shuttle which weaves ruin,
and even the flames, like the tongue of a god
who sucks us up at leisure
until he feels the taste of ash between his teeth.

WITH A LITTLE EFFORT

In order to beat the iron
you must first have an anvil
and our bodies over it
deafened by vibrant hammering.
That's how I loved you when forging my tools.

With a little effort
it's the same for the intellect
or for God
beating out his angels
deafened by vibrant hammering.

JUST A DAY

A day
means almost nothing
in the middle of the street
with feet immersed in the rose garden
I go towards the house
beautiful fingernails in the darkness
light up headlamps of pride.

The earthquake begins
and beauty shows its entrails
caressing the walls of a house now destroyed.

Just a day, and metaphysics is a ploughed field,
the rubble brings forth buds.

TESTING THE TEMPERATURE
OF THE WATER

The room seems ever deeper
as though pushed down by your steps
as if you were sinking between the walls
and sinking them with you.

The eye loses and adores you
from the window nearest the door,
the floor swallows you up now
as you bend to put a shoe on your bare foot.

The air welcomes, makes way, creates a void for you
divides easily, closes silently
over the body testing the temperature of the water
for the bath of the child just born.

IT'S NATURAL FOR ME
TO SEE IT LIKE THIS

Just as it's natural for me to see
life covered by a colourless glaze, varnished,
and under it a child, always throbbing in the womb,
its fists beating even now on a drum that can be
soundless

I can't name the woman bearing him,
her thin sacred skin or even the crystal
in which things rest, in that damp cradle,
for I'm puzzled that everything I hold in my hand
is at the same time everything that's taken from me.

LILIANA URSU was born in Sibiu in July 1949. A graduate in English of Bucharest University she has translated from English into Romanian and vice versa. She has also published to date four volumes of her own verse and received critical acclaim in 1980 when she was awarded the Poetry Prize of the Writers' Union. She also writes for children and currently works for Romanian Radio as an editor of cultural programmes. In 1982 she translated from Romanian an anthology of verse, *Fifteen Young Romanian Poets*. She has also translated English and American writers into Romanian.

UNFORGETTING

I put snow
I place silence
Between us.
And in the towns they don't know
Why it's such a bad winter.
My angels
Drink whisky from tall tumblers
And forget to forget you.
Pleasant music
settles gently on my eyelids.
The hour a frightened bird
Settles
Between these walls
All around me
Raised by you
Like a monastery
And I
A soldier loyal
To my solitude
Slide into a white sleep.

AN EARLIER WOUND

Don't unwind the wool too fast—say the old folk.
And look, on the spun thread a ladybird climbs
crimson and exact its path, up into the sky.

The earth still carries my steps,
impatiently you want to unravel the thread.
See how the leaf weighed down with autumn,
doesn't yet leave a single mark on our flesh
loving.

Only the street corner where we met,
desolate under a July sun hot as the Mediterranean,
leaves a tiny mark on the retina—an earlier wound.

DIANA'S SHADE

I don't celebrate you with roses in my hair
or with torches.
Irreverently I gather a few herbs,
and with these greet you today.
The Sabbath light on my face
is just an illusion
and I get tired watching you
and fall asleep at your feet
until your hounds chase me to the dawn.

Oh, as these pressed flowers once knew the sun
my body once knew joy.

HEADS OR TAILS

A Sunday feeling—your face passed through filters of
memory—
like suspicious luggage at airports:
There comes to mind: the fisherman on the wooden
bridge,
golden fish paying with their lives—for a moment's
food
and the pensioner always pacing out the same room,
always the same loneliness.

I no longer lose myself in the tall grass,
on the colt's trail,
—heads or tails—
how the light fails about me,
yet another sign.

COUPLE

By the light of a paraffin lamp two old people fry fish.
Their heads meet only above the pan.
The story of this canvas' day and night
is best known to the ivy on the wall—
for the Master's long grown tired of it.

CIRCUIT

A thin boy, in suit and tie, filing, filing.
Through the dirty windows pigeons watch him.
And he watches them through the lonely window of his
                                                    glasses.
Each surveys the other.
Like a conjurer he plucks a packet of sandwiches
from his black briefcase.
In the catacombs of the future
his slender bones
will be counted, filed.
Some handsome youngsters or just youngsters will
                                        study them
while one of them does the filing another will be
                        fondling the breast of a blonde
while yet another opens his pocket of sandwiches
and takes a bite.

STAGE DIRECTIONS

When the fog lifts I shan't see you any more.
How the days deceive us one by one,
how loneliness scratches at the door!

I make myself another coffee, walk to the four cardinal
                                                    points
of the room. I see nothing.
Hidden behind nylon curtains, always watching,
the sweet nothings of existence don't give me the right
to look at the diamond-like light on the hill.
Only in the beam of head-lights shine
the contours of doves, the dance of love
happy for just a moment.

When the fog lifts a red stain
grows from their scattered flight.
Then life returns to normal.

Scene 2: The cloud of a poem amongst busy streets,
               amongst cups of coffee and whispers.
               A shooting star, a shooting star
               falls on a meadow.
               The hill grows dark then disappears.

INTERRUPTED POEM

We all attempt to do something with our evenings,
                                    with our nights
so we can stuff future ones with souvenirs of the past
like some stuffed bird, beautiful or just frightening
and most of the time we don't even recognise them any
                                    more—
for instance
I'm wondering if I'll ever remember tonight
when I watched a stupid film on T.V.
made myself tea laced with rum,
translated Pound and Dylan Thomas
and watched the face of my son, flushed with dreams
smiling from a far off country
more real than my sterile sadness,
which grins cynically from this poem.

Liliana Ursu

LESS THAN TEN COMMANDMENTS

To concentrate my verse like the Greeks who with a ray
of sun
set ships aflame.
Not to look backwards. Nor at your palm.
To go up to the mountains even if I do meet a birds'
cemetery on the way.
Not to hide when the ink of solitude
blackens my body.
To show you how my hair changes to the rarest colour only
when *you* look at it.
To learn the quick and salty taste of self-knowledge,
To be able to look at the shot bird and understand how
the claw
that strangles my words is her sister.
To smile at you from the helmet of the moon
drunk with the idea of freedom.
(However I wouldn't turn the other cheek even to my
neighbour).

Liliana Ursu

FRAGMENT

With silent voices they sing
they defend themselves
admit their faults
donate their blood
swear at darkness
sweat at the light
and yet
they are born.